"*Distance Sequenc*[...]
queerness, gender, a[...]
like poetry, Luke Suth[...]
embodiment and wild longing that I won't soon [forget.]"

—Mecca Jamila Sullivan, author of *Big Girl*

Photographs, letters, and notebook pages
© 2024 Luke Sutherland

Any Other City excerpt © 2023 Hazel Jane Plante.
Make the Golf Course a Public Sex Forest! sticker © 2023 Maitland Systems Engineering.
Maps and illustrations © National Park Service
(17 U.S.C.§ 403), except where otherwise stated.
No claim to original U.S. Government works.

Distance Sequence
Luke Sutherland

All rights reserved. No part of this publication may be reproduced, stored in a retrieval system or transmited in any form or by any means, electronic, mechanical, photocopying, recording or otherwise without the prior permision of the publisher or in accordance with the provisions of the Copyright, Designs and Patents Act 1988 or under the terms of any license permitting limited copying issued by the Copyright Licensing Angency.

Published by: Neon Hemlock Press
Cover Design by: dave ring

ISBN-13: 979-8-89587-601-5

Luke Sutherland
DISTANCE SEQUENCE

**WINNER OF THE 2023 OUTWRITE CHAPBOOK COMPETITION
SELECTED BY MECCA JAMILAH SULLIVAN**

DISTANCE SEQUENCE

LUKE SUTHERLAND

*"The look on your face yanks my neck on the chain,
and I would do anything to see you again."*
— *Neko Case*

CONTENTS

PRELUDE TO CASCADES
1

MEMORYWORK 1
3

DIALOGUE
8

AN INCOMPLETE OVERVIEW OF ALL THE NEEDLES THAT HAVE ENTERED MY BODY
18

GOLDIE'S LEGS
22

SEATTLE CYCLE
26

MEMORYWORK 2
42

TOP EDGES TO EDGE ON / 46
NURSELOG / 54
TIDEPOOL / 60
RAINSHADOW / 68

BREAKER, BREAKER
73

FLOATING BRIDGE
76

BACKCOUNTRY REMEMBERINGS
80

MEMORYWORK 3
82

ABOUT THE AUTHOR / 88
ABOUT THE PRESS / 88

PRELUDE TO CASCADES

IT'S NOT COLD until it is, and then we are gathering up empties and dousing the embers with a cauldron of water, cast iron and heavy, a weight that feels good in the hands.

The others have already left, and upstairs B asks if I want tea, of course I do, yes; in their bedroom I step over discarded foam earplugs and peel off layers and watch them busy themself.

Watch their beautiful hair, which is blonde which is red which is gold.

B fills an electric kettle with water from the bathroom sink and tells me how it can't run at the same time as the space heater even though it is cold, trust me, it's cold.

When the water boils they steep it in an iron pot, and soon a cup scalds my hands.

I hold it anyway, fingertips tented and spidery around the hot metal, sip as we sit close together on a bed without pillows, just a quilt and delicate patterned sheets and a mattress I will lose an earring to, drink one cup two cups three with them refilling and us talking about something, something.

About how I am a man, sort of, about how they're learning that they are not.

Later we will spend hours wringing the pulp from each other, heads resting in the cradle of our armpits, no pillows, Prine singing and the Cascadian flag shadowing our bodies.

But first I watch them eat dried tea leaves straight out of the jar.

That can't taste good I say and they tell me to try it so I do, brittle bitter bones turning plump on my tongue, and when I slosh water around my mouth to loosen the paste from my teeth, when later our mouths meet and gush and mend, it becomes its own kind of tea.

MEMORYWORK 1

I HAVE NEVER TRIED to remember anything the way I am trying to remember you. There are consequences to remembering. My head is crowded with exit wounds. Thoughts bleed at the worst times. I try to remember, but keep getting lost on my way back to you. This archive is unorganized. You never know which file might come up.

Clothes used to stick to my wounds, B. I haven't told you that yet. Undressing, degloving, it was the same. My elbows and knees were always weeping. If I sat still long enough, fabric flush against my broken skin, they would start to fuse. The crack wanted to close, and I was tight as a drum in those spots.

To move again, to stretch my limbs straight, god, to walk, it was violent as drought, it was scorched earth cruelty. I dreaded nakedness. Peeling off clothes was an eruption, the shock of it so bracing, it killed everything else.

On our last day, we dressed in each other's clothes, drove back to Seattle, and paid for a room in a stinking hotel. The glare of departing airplanes was hot in the windows, the water was hot in our shared bath. We switched shirts again, twice: once before falling into the sleepless bed, for the smell of each other, and again in the morning before you dropped me off at my gate.

TSA agents looked at me strangely, and was it because of my sobbing, my fagdyke folly, the anomaly of my body? You texted me as I went through security:

Can't drive right now /

Wish I could have spent an hour crying into your jacket

Now, at home, I pull on jeans I haven't worn since I was with you, the ones that used to be M's, my other love. Our closet is full of these exchanges. A dress that I'd worn to a high school dance—lacey with puff shoulders and sequins, purchased at a discount from my retail job—is their favorite.

The jeans are long on me, the dress short on them. Changing doesn't hurt anymore.

M came downstairs recently in black denim cutoffs.
I loved wearing those, I said.
Oh right, they replied, looking down.
These used to be yours. I had forgotten.

I uncuff my jeans. Out falls pebbles from La Push, from when I ate shit trying to jump the river you forded so easily, and it may as well be your hair, it may as well be your teeth, B, scattering across my bedroom floor.

I am dreaming of ways to bleed on purpose,
of opening myself under a needle or a knife;
how giving, how gushingly real—

Have you considered that you might be a girl?

Are you shy or just not that interested?
The way you've looked at me before, —

DIALOGUE

1.

Outside their empty apartment. Exterior, day. We are standing by the driver-side door of my car. I had helped them pack a U-Haul with skis, miscellaneous bags and boxes, a set of cast iron pans. B delayed their departure, then delayed again, and again. We took breaks to lay in bed, to buy bread, crusty and wonderful. I open the car door, anguish in my belly. B sees it, in a way, and asks,

Are you cold?

No. I'm just really sad.

Yeah. Shit. Fuck—

—and I don't regret the kiss, and I don't know if this is the last one, and I don't tell anyone how I cry on the drive home, pathetic, halfway delusional, certain I have lost something before it even began.

2.

Before: In B's bed, naked. İnterior, night.

I want to experience the full range of human expression, so it would only make sense to try being femme for a while.

I don't tell them what they sound like, saying anything to justify a desire except admitting that they might want it at all.

Would I have been happier as a cis woman? Maybe.   Probably. But that's not quite it either.

They want to know how to *know*. They want certainty like a long pull of water. They want me to call it for them. So when they say maybe, I say

Yes, maybe.

Why not? Why not want something?

3.

Before: Outside my apartment. Exterior, night. B unlocks their bike. I watch them, bright lips, elegant brows, pale skin oranged by the lamplight. I already told them how much I would miss them. I already feel crazed from wanting what I barely know.

For the record, you'd be
a very pretty girl.

I'll have to try it sometime.

4.

Before: Downstairs at the gay bar. Interior, night. I ask them to come with me, say placating things about how no one will wonder why they are there on trans night. Say,

I hope this isn't weird,
since you're moving so soon,

before kissing them again. In a week they will drive 2,500 miles away, and I want to know why.

Anyone who has heard me talk for more than ten minutes knows how I feel about the Cascades.

I don't really get it. I've never felt that way about a place before. This land feels like most land. When I'm in traffic on the beltway, when I buy a seltzer at the bodega, aisles heavy with leaning goods, I think about the lack of distinction, how I could be nearly anywhere in the world. B asks me what home feels like. I find myself without an answer.

5.

Before: A bee-themed brewery. Interior, night. We sit across from each other on long wooden benches. Maybe our knees touch. Maybe they are looking at me the way I imagined. B keeps being like

I can't remember the last time
I recognized myself in the mirror,

as though that is a perfectly cisgender thing to say.

Can I kiss you,

I ask as we are saying goodnight, B holding their bicycle intentionally away so it is not between us. They say

yes,

and we do.

6.

Before: B's backyard. Exterior, night. It's cold as fuck. There's a fire, but it's not big enough for all these people. I drink apple cider and talk to strangers about Baltimore and Satanism. My eyes keep looking for B as they float around, playing host. They're cute and a little fucked up, their hair trailing into their whiskey, and when I go to say goodbye, they embrace me so tight it lights up my brain.

Thank you so much for being my friend.

Later, I scroll to the post announcing they have accepted a job on the other side of the country. I look at it for a long time.

7.

Before: Halloween. C's house. Interior, night. When asked,

B says they don't know what their costume is. They look like someone gave them five minutes to get dressed for a renaissance faire in the dark. I've seen them once before, at a different party, and remember them by their hair. I tell them I'm a gay pirate, pointing to the faggy details: my harness, fish hook earring, button that reads **ECSTATIC SODOMITE** in red script.

All I'm missing is a sword.

At what point does a knife become a sword?

They rustle their clothes and pull out a pocket knife, flicking the blade open. It's an elegant thing, French-made with a wooden hilt soft from use. I admire it for a moment.

When it can no longer fit in your pocket.

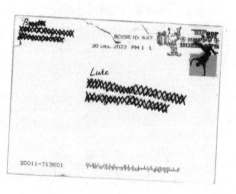

AN INCOMPLETE OVERVIEW OF THE NEEDLES THAT HAVE ENTERED MY BODY

- Thin, wobbling reeds that sway where the acupuncturist plants them on my feet, brow ridge, chin, in the conched folds of my ear

- A thick gauge puncturing cartilage, two silver studs floating in my earlobes

- The tip of a sewing needle, heated first on the stove, then bursting a blister; another suspended painlessly through the thick callus on the pad of my thumb

- 0.5 mL syringe of testosterone cypionate delivered weekly into belly fat

- A phlebotomist prodding the thick meat of my inner elbow, readjusting the tourniquet, failing to find a vein, and finally resorting to an entry site on top of my left hand; it hurts more than all the others

- Preloaded syringes of dupilumab, a monoclonal antibody blocking interleukin 4 and interleukin 13, stored in the fridge and taken biweekly

- The jab of vaccines, two of them administered in the Atlantic City Convention Center, a cavernous hall full of FEMA agents, uniformed officers and of course civilians, all of us patients in one way or another. I sit for twenty minutes in a folding chair, waiting to see how my body will react

→ A quick purr of the tattoo gun subsuming ink into me for the first time, a thrill I wish lasts longer, just three steady lines that form a triangle above my knee

→ Drawing blood into a bag that a nurse then massages, dissolving ozone into plasma before hanging the bag above my head and letting it drip back into me; the feel of it reentering, icy and indescribable

→ Epinephrine, three times: once by a paramedic, once by my mother, once by my college roommate, high as fuck, saving my life in the awful apartment we shared

→ A sterilized needle pushing through a pinch of flesh between my nipple and my collar bone, parallel to the scar, beveled tip pointed up. I do it on my own. I wish someone else would. I close my eyes to imagine that lover, who would be soft with all the sharp things. *Do I want more*, they'd ask, another needle in hand, blood spilling in smooth ribbons—

→ Yes   Yes   Yes

Since we can't send cock over USPS, I think for now we're stuck with notes.

GOLDIE'S
LEGS

I'VE BEEN WAITING to do a piercing scene with this dyke for months, but still my blood remains under my skin. With B, I watch *Foxfire* over Facetime, and the stick n poke scene nearly knocks me out. I want to lick Jenny Shimizu's shorn head. I want to warp through the screen to give Angelina Jolie a hormone prescription and a sub-q lesson.

B's laugh crackles like embers over the line. Their face floats in the corner of the screen, next to the movie. I like to watch them watching. Their image swims with pixels, like my vision does after going from a very bright room into a dark one, corneas straining for purchase. This is the only way we see each other anymore. We've developed habits, like saying *there is something I want to tell you,*

but only   in person.

In the movie, Angelina starts with herself. She outlines the curl of a flame above her breast, filling it in with stabs of yellow and red. The other girls watch, waiting their turn. Girls dance to the Cramps, girls tattoo themselves to Mazzy Star, girls beat the shit out of father/teacher/abuser. Angelina is always there, pretty as a boy, a blade.

B carries a knife like a talisman, or a fidget toy, nicking themself on occasion. I have one too, the same brand. M gave it to me for Christmas. I love the feel of it in my hand, the satisfying snap it makes when I flip out the blade. Sometimes, on calls like this, B and I both hold up our knives as if it means something.

there is something I want to tell you,

but   not yet.

A different call. I pick up and hear the wind whooshing from their lungs. On the ride to a show, through snowy hills

I have only seen on google maps, they swerved their bike to avoid a close call with a car. Gravel buried in their palms. *Thank god you're okay*, I say. And they are, sort of. I stay on the line while they roll their bike back home, while the door opens and the sound of falling into a bed I can't see distorts through the speaker. Their breaths come short and gasping. I'm sewing a poem into a sheet of cardstock, the needle punching through the paper in loud tacks. We listen to each other for a while. Sharp gasp, sharp stitch.

there is something I want to tell you—

I don't bring my knife to the airport. It wouldn't make it past TSA, and I'm already nervous about my hormones. They make me stand in the body snatching machine. Months ago, agents forced M through twice, groping them after. I stood and watched the state assert itself over their body. I stand now, arms up and legs apart, and try not to think of what button they're pressing. I try to imagine Jenny and Angelina and the girls. I imagine your face flushed, unpixelated, hearing what I need you to hear.

It's not really my place to tell you about ~~myself~~ yourself but I think it would've helped me a lot if someone had just given me the option, raised the possibility, even if it didn't stick for me right away...

    I hope you consider, at least

SEATTLE
CYCLE

1.

IT GOES LIKE this: first, we fuck. What else would we do with a room and a bed and a sudden collapse of distance? To be there, against one another, it's almost too much. What I will remember: knocking the heap of decorative pillows to the floor, cool tile on bare feet, releasing a muscle long held, the feel of B, perfect—

In the rental, there's a dresser shaped like a fish. Its eye is an empty drawer. We take turns draping our backs over the curved wood—why, I'm not sure. It's not very comfortable. The room is decorated with blown up pictures of people's bare legs. One wall in the shower is made completely of bricks. There are small boat propellers scattered in the front yard.

B needs more sleep than what we got, and so I lay next to them and read Hazel Jane Plante while they nap. Before the trip, I described our situation to a friend as "*Nevada* in reverse." B had moved across the country, *them* driving away from *me*, when it should've been the other way around. It didn't really make sense, but still, I couldn't help but feel like the Maria to B's James, to imagine myself as some transsexual prophet here to say hey, let me save you some time. How badly I needed, years ago, to hear that my body was possible. To have my shame turned inside out.

I move to the couch. B's shape is mounded under the comforter, and I watch the warmth of dreams twitch through them.

Plante writes:

The first time I fucked you and was inside of you, the first time I fucked you without my fingers or a toy, that first time, I kept thinking of waves, of a dolphin undulating in the ocean. Maybe that helped me feel okay about being inside of you. And the way your eyes kept looking into mine also made it feel okay, made it feel good, so gushingly good. Your eyes, my eyes. An ocean, a dolphin. And, oh fuck. Fuck. My body crashing again and again against the waves of your body.

The blinds half drawn, the street so quiet. I start writing notes, not knowing what they will become. Half the pages of my notebook are pinched shut by a paperclip, years I don't want to revisit. My old name is written in the front. These are things I would rather not address.

B stirs, their hair a red cloud I want to wring the rain out of. Our eyes meet across the tile.

You left me, they say.

I'm right here.

Not close enough.

2.

Time passes—one moment transforms

                                                  into the other.

Pointing to every mountain,
        is that it? Is that?

                                                  → RAINIER REVEAL

A kiss at Pony, wallpapered by porn

                                                  → *DYKEFAG FOLLY*

Tongues unfurl, a finger inside,
        bare feet on tile

                                                  → FUCKING FAIRIES

    We're early for the DIY show, so we hole up in the bar next door. I get a gin and tonic way too strong for me, baby that I am, and we sit close enough to wear each other's skin. B douses tater tots in Tabasco. Near us, two people with black smeared across their eyes drink quietly. Butches hug each other by the door. Everyone in this city looks like a queer, and I'm not complaining.

The show space starts to fill. It's all ages, and we're surrounded by young metalheads so stylish it hurts. There's amps stacked against walls, a soup of cables snaking the floor. VVILFRED is setting up, and it's the two from the bar with the heavy makeup, the bassist and the singer. A girl takes off her strappy boots and walks stocking-footed across the cement floor. The band, tuned and poised, starts to play.

Sludgy distortion oozes over our heads. The band is tight. Propulsive drums, muscular bass, a screeching guitar. The bassist's eyes cut to the singer, the drummer, bright white against dark makeup. The crowd thrashes. I love how sound compels my body. I love watching B, their long braid whipping about. The singer growls:

> *I would let you break all my limbs*
>
> *I would let you peel off my skin*

It's a hell of a set, but I'm tired, I'm so fucking tired, so we don't stick around. Out front, another trans person tells me they like my patches and pins. I like you, you. I love every transsexual even when I don't. B and I start to climb the steep streets back towards the rental, arms knotted together. A sticker on the back of a traffic sign says:

- - - - - - - - -
SISSIES RULE
- - - - - - - - -

and I have to agree.

Thigh burning inclines, talking dykehood and
warm sex,
cold beer, hot nuts
Pony up
with cock and eyeballs
spinning from the ceiling, transsexual
dick winking from above
me
exuberant fags, Sunday night scary
sounds, its ~~really~~ raining of course
and we kiss anyway
with slicked brows, feet worn
down to meat and bone,
a bed not ours

3.

Rhododendron shades the sidewalk, the bulbs wound tightly as puckering fists, a shiver of fuschia hidden inside. Flowers and faggots go hand in hand, but the city isn't blooming,

                                                  not yet.

    The telephone poles in Cap Hill are plastered inches thick with wheatpaste flyers. Punk shows, sex parties, dozens of ads for a movie we've both already seen. If we see it again, B says, we could fool around in the back row. That's what you do when you have a boyfriend,

                                                      right?

    I could peel back the flyers like dermal layers, like how illness excavated me. The loose corners are tempting. I did this as a child, too: digging my nails under a shingle of bark, hinging it away from the tree; underneath, the bizarre fuzz of a caterpillar. I resist

                                                  the urge.

    We're downtown and both desperate for a bathroom. Turned away in a hotel lobby, we scuttle across the street to the convention center. There are two stalls in the men's room, but something is wrong, and not in the way it usually is. A man's head and shoulders are visible above the walls of his stall. We can see each other

completely.

    I can't make sense of it, a person's face where there should be only a wall, but god do I need to go, and so I step inside the other stall and turn the latch. I look towards the man. The laminate wall dividing our stalls only reaches as high as my nipples, privacy an impossibility. Piss sleets against urinals. I balk, needing to be emptied but not known, grasping for the dick I don't have, at least not in the way he would expect. Not in the way I pretend I don't

want.

    I leave without pissing. We keep walking. The buildings get taller and the telephone poles clearer. Flowers, but only on a florist's stand. Of course I think of M always finding pansies to eat, chewing the petals like evergreen gum. I imagine it, all of us walking together somehow, the two of them chewing and me,

loving.

At the harbor I tell B how I thought it was a mirror at first, when I looked across the bathroom and saw the man. We're headed towards the water, entangling in each other at every red light. I try to remember the first time I used the men's room, or the last time I used the women's, and find that I can't. Would it have been better to use the women's? Would they have looked at me the way I looked at the man? In some ways, I am more afraid of women than men;

                                                                     but not many.

> Make the Golf Course a Public Sex Forest! Room full of dyke fags, the generative potential of erotica, how its constraints force us to write beyond the imagination......

4.

THERE'S A RABBIT on the way home from the erotica reading. It rests the globe of its body in the grass, round in that way rabbits can get, and pays us no mind. We stand there and fuss for a while. Before B left the east coast, I painted a rabbit on a rock for them. They'd told me how much they loved seeing the creatures, delighted by twitching cheeks, flattened ears. B made a point of showing me the rock on their dresser when I first spent the night. They called me, halfway through the cross country drive, with it rattling on the dashboard.

It's too early for cherry blossoms or huckleberries. Rain mists, but barely falls. I'm dizzy with dykelove and the generative potential of the erotic. I want to desecrate a golf course. I want to write beyond my imagination. Instead, we keep walking home towards a bed

                                                        not ours.

A street that ends in a staircase

↓   sodium yellow streetlights

        cars parked at strange angles

↓   Rainier, unseen but hulking

                kissing again against a garden wall

↓   it's a good one, alright—

5.

Ducks in the Japanese gardens, sun soaked and paired,
curl their necks into themselves and keep their eyes closed
to tourists. We will never know the pleasure of tucking beak
under wing, but oh, B—
                this might get close enough:
evergreens, vines, cloaks of moss and low-cover bamboo,
paperbark exfoliating in ribbons.
    We take turns photographing each other on a bridge low
over the water. If there are koi in the pond, we don't see any.
I wish their gilded bodies and gulping mouths would roil
the surface, eager and needing. The kind of hunger I could
recognize. To god:

Please,   *when we cross the bay,*   *let us see whales.*

On the ferry we leave the car, eat cinnamon rolls on the deck, and let the wind whip our faces. The bay is ecstatic as Seattle crawls away. The sound of B's camera is lost behind the rush of water, the ripping engine. I look at them looking. The lens hides their face. Their hair flies.

Keep this wind in my lungs forever,   please,   don't let it end.

We finally spot Rainier then, hazy but unmistakable.

She's so beautiful,   I hardly know   what to say.

MEMORYWORK 2

IN MIDDLE SCHOOL, a teacher passed out coffee stirrers and instructed us to breathe through them. We put the plastic between our lips, sealed our noses shut, and rasped for thin plumes of air. I think this was to say that we should never smoke. Or maybe it was to simulate asthma.

Did they have you do this too, B? Tell me, what was the lesson for?

Panic creeps spider-like down both my arms. It's shimmering, long-legged and cool. My eyes stop telling the truth. Unreality, a screen I watch from deep in my mind. These are not my hands, my wrists, my thighs. This is not my meaty tongue. This is not my throat constricting pipe cleaner thin. I am remembering something on the cellular level, and I want it to stop.

Of the times I thought I might die, the one before graduation was the worst. I got close to telling you once, but embarrassment overwhelmed me. How typically pathetic of me to asphyxiate from a bong. How terrible to doubt that it was real at all—J told me later that he watched my lips turn blue. It was before we broke up, before the hospital debt collector called and the nights I kept myself awake to the point of collapse, the feeling of falling asleep too close to death. It's not something I enjoy telling. But here is how it happened:

Class is canceled on the day a bong almost kills me. We talk of sledding and blanket forts. My friends make chocolate chip pancakes (which I cannot eat) and, later, pack a bowl in our dark semi-basement apartment. I want to be with them in a way I'm usually not, so when J finishes I ask him for a hit.

He has to light it for me. I cough a lot.

It's normal, it's fine, and I go to pull on jeans I can barely feel. My friends are already gloved and jacketed by the door. It's time to go sledding. I watch as the ceiling lamp turns a stab of violent yellow, right next to the leak that sometimes gushes like an open wound; I catch sight of snow out the window so white it vibrates, my friends call me, my throat swells, vision cleaves, legs gummy—

    the edges of my mind soften

                                and pool

        into syrup

like a bowl of macerated   berries.

I pinch my thighs, gnash my thick tongue into hamburger. I need the pain to hold me. My friend shoots me full of epinephrine while the rest of them watch. A needle in the leg is not unfamiliar, and yet—

                it is never quite the same.

Paramedics ask too many questions. When they carry me out, I see the snow again. It dusts my legs as I'm laid on the gurney (I've been here before), bright and movie-set thick and painting Irving Street white.

Nothing has ever been so beautiful. Nothing will ever be beautiful again.

Top Edges To Edge On

THE LARGEST LOG YOU CAN FIND

along a shallow but wide river, the bank dropping quick below your dangling feet and the rainforest to your backs. The tread of your boots are ribbed with moss, your hair is like moss. You can wed your lover in a cathedral of lichen, you can stay on the log, bestride the bark red as raw steak, flaking against your thighs like tender salmon. Don't forget to pluck your glasses from where they slide into the river in the heat of the moment, gray metal on smooth, alluvial rock.

Olympic National Park

Pacific Silver Fir
Abies amabilis

Sea anemones
Anthopleura xanthogrammica

THE LIP OF A GROTTO HIGH ABOVE

a rocky beach which you scramble hand to hand over algae slicked boulders to reach. Find footholds in the outcrops, straddle hips, let the sun bleach your eyelids as they close. Think about falling. Take breaks to spot sea stars, urchins, giant green anemones in the bowls of seawater below.

Consider the grotto's pool, dim with bacteria and bird shit, but turn back to your lover. Finish before high tide.

Protect
and wil
wild a
safe dis
pets on

A SNOWBANK WELL OFF THE TRAIL

that covers your knees in quick bites, cold and soft swallowings. Take turns on your back, switching before the damp stains your skin. Listen to snow tumble from overburdened branches. Trace a finger along the peaks of the dogtooth horizon. Before trudging back to the trail, take a steaming piss that melts the snow between your legs.

---

urself, your pet by not feeding als, keeping a and not taking trails.

Footprints can leave lasting scars. Help preserve the meadows by staying on snow or designated trails.

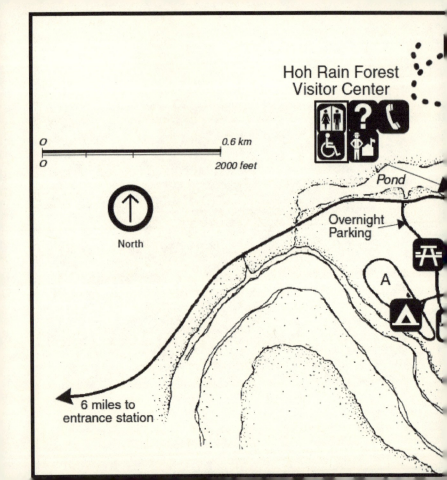

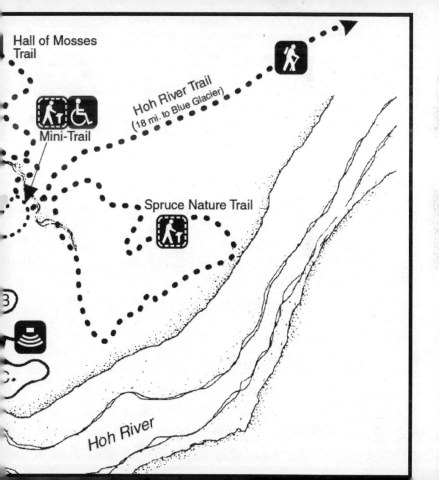

Nurselog

I TAKE MY SHOT in the Hoh rainforest, making sure B gets a good angle with the little disposable camera I'd bought at CVS. I'm always forgetting at home, letting days go by before realizing I missed a dose, but here I'm buzzing for it.

My hiking bag is a temporary med kit: alcohol swabs, syringes, bandaids, two gauges of needles. I'm used to injections. Pinching the fat of my stomach, angling the needle, the one-two-three-go before the puncture. I rotate hormone days with monoclonal antibody ones.

I forget about those shots, too.

The Hall of Mosses loop is short, but we spend hours on it anyway. The air is damp in my lungs, spiked with licorice fern. Lichen overwhelms the landscape. The branches of douglas-firs and Sitka spruces hang heavy with a fur of algaes.

Signs along the path are lyrical and strangely charged:

> *[moldering logs, trunks shaggy with moss]*
>
> *[plant on plant]*
>
> *[lush beards of clubmoss]*

And it's true, the lush shag of it all is romantic, bacteria and fungi fucking all around us. Lichens like leaves, like cracked paint, like gunpowder. B bends their head to inspect the composite, and their hair sheeted over their face looks like a red shrub of fruticose anchored to the bark.

    I pick a spot just off the trail and lay out my supplies on a log, the glass vial of T nestled into decaying wood. I swab a spot just below my belly button while a family snakes down the path.

I slide the needle into the vial and invert it, pulling thick liquid into the syringe, flicking out pockets of air. B is kneeling in the moss with the camera raised. I can hear the many small voices of the family. The point of the needle lingers over my stomach. There's murmuring, a shower of boot disturbed dirt. I try not to notice them noticing me; I've spent years practicing, but I'm not very good at it. When I finally inject, B peaks around the camera to say I look metal as hell.

The needle draws out a coin of blood as it exits my body. It sits there, tense, a blot of red amongst a stream of freckles. N, the first trans man I ever knew, taught me to hold the used syringe over my finger and squeeze the plunger one last time, swiping those precious drops across my upper lip and jaw. It helps the hair grow, he said. I have no idea if this is true. I do it anyway, always, and it is the anointment that makes me whole.

The family is gone, maybe not knowing what they saw. B embraces me, and I forget it all. I love how they witness me. I love that they know which mountains are which. I love the sound they make when they are surprised. I love how they love the forest. I love that they stopped the car the moment we saw elk. I love when they lean their head into my hand. I love that they refuse to eat anything I can't. For a few minutes, there is only this.

TRANS FEAR

When is the right time to leave? [*always*]
Is there ever a right time [*never*]
What does that mean? [*agony*]
Where would we go? [*together*]
Who would take us? [*arms outstretched*]
Do we wait until the killings? [*it's too late*]
Do we wait until it's one of our friends? [*no*]
Could we live through that vigil? [*no*]
Which of us might bury
      ourselves preemptively? [*yes*]
Do we count ourselves lucky? [*…*]
How could we leave, knowing who can't? [ ]

  We spend a long time in the trees, on a tree, by the river. We kiss, for lack of answers. I use their knife to carve **FAG4DYKE** into the wood. Which of us is which is a matter of opinion.

&ON

Much, much later, a man—a coworker of mine, my building opposite his—will tell the audience at a work event that trans people are pedophiles. He doesn't say it like that exactly, but we all know what he means. I will feel rattled, sick, jaded. I will file complaints. I will despair. I will consider quitting all of the time. I will look up the cost of my prescriptions without insurance. Later.

Still in the forest, B and I stand in front of a plaque telling us that we are looking at a nurselog. The massive trunk lays prone on the floor. Nooks of its body collect detritus. Moss, needles, leaf litter and squirrel shit—a mattress of lush humus for sprouting seedlings. A colonnade of mature hemlocks straddle the log from which they grew. In another spot, the nurselog has rotted away completely. Nutrients cycle, burls break down. Its children stand on tented roots, hollow air where their parent used to be, not able to let go of the shape.

A nurselog is like a whale fall. A nurselog is like a transsexual living past their life expectancy.

Have I ever told N that he made my life possible? That I'm still on stilts, alive over the space he made?

Tidepool

THERE'S A MOMENT when I am alone with it, the view of Ruby Beach. I can see the water churning around submerged boulders from between shadowed, wispy pines. A creek twines into the ocean. An island off the coast sprouts a garland of trees. It's beautiful in a way that makes everything feel more and less real. My phone dead, I pull out the disposable camera and take a picture, thumb pushing down on the plastic button until the shutter snaps.

And then B is with me again, arm lacing through mine. They want me to see a sunset like the ones they grew up with, the star sinking into the sea, not like the east coast where you have to wake before dawn to witness the two kiss. I want to see B at their most beautiful. I want to see everything that has ever been beautiful to them.

The beach is like a timber yard. Massive logs of driftwood splay across stones, limbs blunted, bark bleached silver.

Olympic National Park

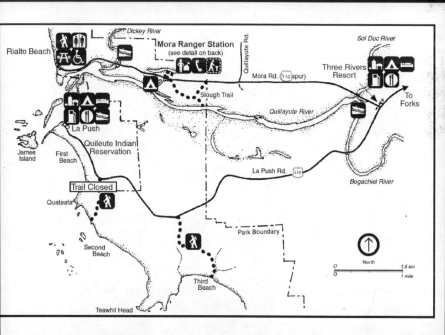

We have to scrabble over them to reach the water. B, they roll their pants over their calves and walk into the surf, leaning forward to brace against a cold wave.

It's foam and haze, oceanic spittle, the cloud-laden horizon swelling like the tide; the sun shyly, out of sight.

I catch the eyes of another beachgoer. We are trying to read transness into each other's bodies. Or at least I am. They're tall and slim, bobbed hair tucked into the collar of a nylon windbreaker. There's the familiar nod, the gentle look.

They say a soft hello. B and I wait our turn as they climb the roots of a log, a Western Hemlock blown down by wind, washed down river, and carried back onto the shore. A partner takes the maybe-trans person's picture from below. I wish, desperately, that I could see it.

INTERTIDAL ETIQUETTE
— DO —

- Run fingers through salt thickened hair
- Eat crackers (mostly turned to dust) on a sunny dome of rock
- Point out sea stars, colored plum or tangerine, for B to swivel their lens towards
- Crouch over tidepools, admire gooseneck barnacles, periwinkles, neon eel-grass, chiton,
- limpets, an unknown species of fish
- Pet a dog named Pigeon
- Run over sun warmed pebbles, jump into each other's arms, fall, get up, climb the
- logs, pose, embrace
- Admire lesbians having their wedding photos taken by the sea, the butch
- resplendent and comforting in their fitted suit
- Climb the rocks higher, then higher still
- Imagine the abundance of a forest underwater, kelp undulating and octopus morphing

— DON'T —

- Fumble while jumping the river, plunging knee deep in cold water, damp jeans for the day
- Leave your phone amongst the pebbles, by the feet of a dog named Pigeon
- Believe high tide won't come for you

ALL THE WATER'S A STAGE

PICK UP A tough tube of kelp, the stipe of the giant plant, and can hardly believe its solidity. I had recently written a story set in a kelp forest, about a dyke falling in love with an octopus. Holding the stipe, feeling its unwillingness to yield as I squeeze it in my hand, how plastic-like it is, I wonder if I got it all wrong. I wanted to write about the illusion of documentary, the way narrative obscures as often as it reveals. About the way the non-human is always a vessel, never an agent, of meaning.

I don't know what all this documenting is for, but still, B and I take pictures of each other in all manner of scenes, as if the image could feel anything like their thigh pressed between my legs. Later, I will write, as if the image could smell of fried tortillas or cum, taste like brine or cider or the shared glass of water next to the bed.

We find a spot on the sea-facing side of a boulder. It's private and precarious. We touch each other there for a long time. The wind wraps their hair around my face. The way time unspools and horizons melt—I couldn't capture it if I tried.

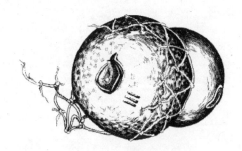

Rainshadow

GLACIAL ERRATICS

From up on Hurricane Ridge, you can see Canada across the Salish Sea. We play in front of the view, this reminder of inept borders. Here the snow falls so thick that it architects the landscape year round. The weight bends trees, preserves permanent meadows. The range itself is the child of ice, formed by the lapping tongues of Pleistocene glaciers that disfigured and reinvented it.

We fall on our asses and knees, throw snow, sing Big Time, two creatures dropped here by forces well beyond us. At least that's how I let it feel. Off screen: the car that drove us up the mountain. The plane that flew me across the country. The caravan, wagon, horse that ferried genocidal settlers West.

Olympic National Park

I am writing as though I am only a passenger in vehicles I have no part in driving. A stone set upon a glacier that will advance and recede according to its own whims. Nature is discrete; I am innocent. These are lies that are easy to tell.

I look at B and wonder, *could they love me like the snow?*—as though love could return land on its own.

OROGRAPHIC LIFT

In bed, post-fuck, tired and talkative, we teach each other about our childhoods. I don't recount the memories with the sharpest edges (my brother, the knife, the underside of the kitchen table), at least not yet. Holding each other, B listening to me the way they do, I know that eventually I will.

B remembers the fights with their father over their hair. I try to imagine how it might've looked back then, curling just past their ears, tickling the nape of their neck. They would always ask why, why should they have to cut it? Their father never had an answer. They always ended up at the barber anyway.

Is there something you're not saying?

B isn't looking at me when they ask it. The bed takes up most of the cabin's dark, tiny room. I press my nose into the musty pillow by their neck. They want to know how to know. They want me to say I think they're really a woman, to grip the bandage for them and tear, get it over with. I try to explain that it's not like that.

They've been on the dry side of the mountain for too long. There are clouds clustered at the summit, heavy with nurturing water. If only B could get there, condense at the dew point, descend down the other side. They would have forests to play in. They would know abundance, as I have.

What do you do once you know you're trans?

What I did was not speak for a very long time. What I did was think about borders and mutilate myself until it felt better. I can feel how hard B is listening. So instead I say,

You should probably try having a lot of sex.

And I really do mean it.

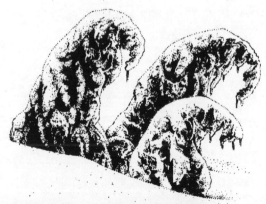

©1977 from *Northwest Trees* by Ramona Hammerly. Reprinted with permission of The Mountaineers Books, Seattle.

That night in the cabin when I slept without my earrings in and you had to re-penetrate my earlobes - for the next month I would feel a little scar bump in my right earlobe from that. It's just now in the last week recovered. I miss having a mark on my body from you. But I'm sure I'm not the same person I was before I met you,

BREAKER BREAKER

BSLEEPS WITHOUT THEIR earrings in, and the holes close overnight. We had just picked out a new pair—two dangling twists of leather, hippie as hell—at a little boutique in Forks the day before.

I loved the swing of them, subtle against B's copper hair.

We stand in the warm glow of the vanity lights. I inspect their lobe, the hole still visible, and work one end of a stud in. Their flesh resists. I hesitate, and they crack their knuckles, the sound echoing through the little cabin.

B has a way of popping the smallest joints in their fingers by gripping the end of each digit and twisting. They've tried to twist mine for me, but my hands are reluctant. Still, we find other ways to share our bones, like when I scoop my chest into upward dog and feel their hands press down on either side of my spine. Like when we admire each other's cracks, the snap of wrists, pop of knees and ankles, saying *good one, god, that one sounded good.*

The earring back slips. It chimes against the sink, and I squat to fish it from the pilly bathroom mat. At their ear again, I ease it in. A bead of fluid pearls as I break skin.

Human blood is vegan, in a way, if everyone involved is into it, but the rule is no cannibalism in the bedroom.

> *Maybe if we were stranded, maybe if one of us died,* B says.
>
> *Maybe. As long as it was for survival and it didn't turn you on.*

I tell them both could be true. *What then?*

Would they drink me if I said yes? Would they deglove flesh with devotion, wear my carpals as earrings, swing their head so when the mountain snow caught the sun, it would reflect off bleached bone too?

B admits that they can't stand sharp things near their face. They haven't cut their hair in nearly a decade. In the bathroom I pierce them anew, and they only flinch a little. We joke about what other wounds I might give them, what new sex could be had, if only we knew what to say.

I would say yes, feast upon me. Make me votive in oblivion. Break me towards pleasure.

FLOATING BRIDGE

WE BOTH AGREE, shower sex is ridiculous, but the cetacean slick of skin on skin, it's what we keep coming back for.

B likes it boiling, even in the summer, so I stay back from the spray and lean against the wall, soaking cool tile into my spine. The ledges are lined with soaps, conditioners, and a cider to share. We take turns sipping, our throats sweet and cold. The hosts stocked the cabin with cheap shampoo, but of course B brought their own, creams with rosehip, kelp, extracts of all kinds. B's red curls reach the divot above their ass, a curtain parting to bare their neck. It takes work, hair like that.

I rub conditioner into their scalp and down the length of a ringlet, kiss shoulder freckles, tug gentle ruptures through the knots. I attempt a fishtail braid, my first in years. Later I demonstrate how to wrap wet hair in an elegant bath towel knot; what is transsexual love without skill exchange?

They are laughing, always, and we live on steam for a while. I try not to count down the days.

In Port Angeles, on a tower above the sea, I cry for the first time. Everyone on the pier is scared of the skyward dykes, processing emotions above their heads. Behind us are mountains we romped down. Ahead, there are big cargo ships, a Coast Guard helicopter, birds that dunk themselves relentlessly into the deep.

I could say something about the parallel of the mechanical and the natural, its relationship to my body (B's body) as made things, how nature doesn't really exist, not in the way we want it to. But the only thought I can spare for the land is how many miles of it will soon be between us.

Briefly, a seal crests, looks about, and dives. B is too slow with their camera.

We share a shower again.

Our car gets stuck on a drawbridge waiting for a sailboat to pass its tall mast. I feel B feeling it.

Not yet, I say, *I'm not gone yet.*
We still have to drive. We have to wait until night.

The other captive passengers stand at the railing, as we do, and stare over the sun-soaked canal. The water is flat and shining. A miracle of dolphins buoys to the surface. One must be a juvenile, its dorsal fin so small, just a knuckle of tissue along its spine. The pod lingers a while. There are maybe a dozen of them, surfacing in lazy circles.

B is ready with the camera. The sound of the shutter parcels time into moments.

Imagine: skin sluicing through Pacific water, a rapturous, limbless life, oh, to soak like that forever, B's hands on my scars, the crest of hips meeting waist—

In the hotel by the airport, we take a cramped bath. They cross their ankles, heels propped against the wall, and I cup their body with mine.

Of course the water is hot. Of course the hair sticks to our foreheads.

And they manage to laugh, yes.

Our skin reddens where the water touches it, ruby floodlines that persist even after we towel off. The steam stretches our pores until we are covered in gulping mouths. I wrap their thick braid around my fist. Not yet, I wish I could say, but it is night.

BACKCOUNTRY REMEMBERINGS
use of counter-balance techniques

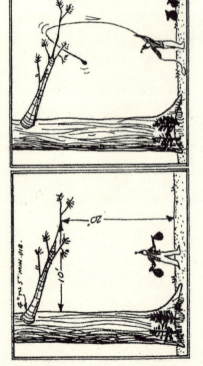

How can I capture it in the amber of my mind?

To give in to a touch, to feel resin where there should be flesh, O, flesh!

BEARS WANT YOUR MIND, TOO!

BACKPACKERS BEWARE!

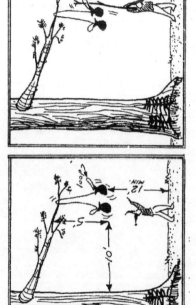

To let the wound fossilize—a blister's fluid unburst and forever hard, Suspended and Lacquer-like.

Fish skin flakers; Memories mineralize.

Veins nestle deeper, silent under webbed scar tissue.

Dream of piercing, of bursting the blister; I break with pleasure at the thought.

GOOD REMEMBERING TAKES PRACTICE
HANG THOUGHTS LIKE FOOD

MEMORYWORK 3

    T tells me about a friend of hers whose boyhood home was infested with carpenter bees. They rasped great tunnels into wood, rotating their mandibles in a circle, sawdust soft in their wake. The bees bore so deep, the boy could hear the beating of wings in his bedroom walls at night.
    Do you think he hears them now, B,
                                  even when they're not there?

    When I got home, I told M I missed them, and I meant it. I tell you I miss you now, and I mean it.

∞

A few weeks apart, and you send me a voice memo that sounds like a mistake, just wind crackling over the line. I play it again. This time I hear faint, chirping voices—a chorus of frogs. The text that follows:

> *Could you hear them? I hope you could. I love you. I wanted to share the experience of there being frogs with you.*

Every rabbit in the grass makes me think of you. Everything, every beautiful thing, is of you.

∞

Months later, I react to a meal I was told was safe. M and I sit in Dupont Circle. People play chess and ride scooters. I feel the spidercrawl of panic when my throat starts to swell. *These are not my legs*, my mind says. *This is not my body.* I check for the epinephrine in my bag over and over, but don't use it.

M holds me on the bench. I love them. I love their tenderness. The episode slowly dissolves. Weeks pass, and I think about killing myself nearly every day.

∞

I remember it now—your body a dewy bloom, tunnel of warm muscle that blinked about my hand as I bore into you, your face buried in the pillow.

Or: lying in the bed you made of your car, the seats down, my eyes in the canopy outside the window, looking at leaves until pleasure forced them closed.
After, using a water bottle to wash me from our fingers.

Or: hand down my pants on the back porch, phone balancing against a shoulder, hearing you hungry, so far away. Crying over the railing afterward.

∞

In the sex club, I watch someone carve an intricate mandala into another's thigh with quick, shallow cuts. I embrace a St. Andrew's cross while leather lashes my chest. A man paints fire across my back, extinguishing it instantly. Pain douses my brain. I laugh because it's funny.

Yes, I need this / this exact thing, Yes

B, when we're together again,

can we hurt in all the right ways?

Promise me. Remember me.

∞

You tell me you are going for a run through the prairies. Hills I've never seen before, might not ever see. Your hair pulled back. Your feet and heart pounding. Sweat and dust and sweat.
I pick up my phone and text you:

I hope the frogs are out tonight.

∞

Walking from work, I hear the gradual fading in and out of insectsound as I pass under blossoming trees along the sidewalk. They're crowded with dozens of bees, most of them a small, nondescript species I can't identify. I watch one pollendrunk with its head in a blossom, back legs peddling the air. A few bumblebees, large and obvious, form fat dollops on the flowers. They drone at a lower pitch than the others. I watch for a while, send you a video. The sound dissipates as I walk like an ambulance speeding away from me.

∞

I tell you about my small deathwish. I don't have to; our lives are separate enough that I could let you go on not knowing. But isn't it enough to be on the other side of the mountain? There is a limit to the distance I can bear. I want you on the rain-soaked side. I want you to grow off me.

My fingers type	→	*This is just something that happens to me sometimes.*
My mind says	→	*theknifetheknifethekni*

the knife. I hold you in the amber of my mind rather than my bed. I kiss M and imagine turning to kiss you too, imagine us three, alive. There is abundance to be had. There is a tide coming in.

Please, let me bleed on purpose.

Let me ache. Let me not forget.

ABOUT THE AUTHOR

Luke Sutherland is a multi-genre writer and library worker. He was a finalist for the Larry Neal Writers' Award, the *Black Warrior Review* Flash Contest, and the *SmokeLong Quarterly* Award for Flash Fiction. His work has appeared in *smoke and mold*, *ANMLY*, *Bright Wall/Dark Room*, and elsewhere. He is also co-editor of the DC-based trans micropress Lilac Peril. This is his debut chapbook.

"Prelude to Cascades" previously appeared in *Stone of Madness*
"Nurselog" previously appeared in *ALOCASIA*
"Tidepool" previously appeared in *Black Warrior Review*

ABOUT THE PRESS

Neon Hemlock is a Washington, DC-based small press publishing speculative fiction, rad zines and queer chapbooks. Learn more about us at www.neonhemlock.com. Find us on Twitter at @neonhemlock.